Th

Florian Zeller is a French novelist and playwright. He won the prestigious Prix Interallié in 2004 for his third novel, *Fascination of Evil*. His plays include *L'Autre*, *Le Manège*, *Si tu mourais*, *Elle t'attend* and *La Vérité*. *La Mère* (*The Mother*, Molière Award for Best Play in 2011) and *Le Père* (*The Father*, Molière Award for Best Play in 2014), starring Robert Hirsch and Isabelle Gelinas (Molière Awards for Best Actor and Actress, Prix du Brigadier in 2015). *Une Heure de tranquillité* (*A Bit of Peace and Quiet*) opened with Fabrice Luchini, and has since been adapted for the screen, directed by Patrice Leconte. *Le Mensonge* (*The Lie*) was staged in 2015 and *L'Envers du décor* opened in January 2016 at the Théâtre de Paris, starring Daniel Auteuil, and *Avant de s'envoler* (*Before it Flies Away*) at the Théâtre de l'Oeuvre in October 2016, starring Robert Hirsch and Isabelle Sadoyan, directed by Ladislas Chollat.

Christopher Hampton was born in the Azores in 1946. He wrote his first play, *When Did You Last See My Mother?*, at the age of eighteen. Since then, his plays have included *The Philanthropist*, *Savages*, *Tales from Hollywood*, *Les Liaisons Dangereuses*, *White Chameleon*, *The Talking Cure* and *Appomattox*. He has translated plays by Ibsen, Molière, von Horváth, Chekhov and Yasmina Reza. His television work includes adaptations of *The History Man* and *Hotel du Lac*. His screenplays include *The Honorary Consul*, *The Good Father*, *Dangerous Liaisons*, *Mary Reilly*, *Total Eclipse*, *The Quiet American*, *Atonement*, *Cheri*, *A Dangerous Method*, *Carrington*, *The Secret Agent* and *Imagining Argentina*, the last three of which he also directed.

FLORIAN ZELLER

The Lie

translated by
CHRISTOPHER HAMPTON

FABER & FABER

First published in 2017
by Faber and Faber Limited
74–77 Great Russell Street, London WC1B 3DA

Typeset by Country Setting, Kingsdown, Kent CT14 8ES
Printed and bound by CPI Group (UK) Ltd, Croydon, CRO 4YY

A CIP record for this book
is available from the British Library

ISBN 978-0-571-34268-6

MIX
Paper from
responsible sources
FSC
www.fsc.org FSC® C013604

2 4 6 8 10 9 7 5 3 1

The Lie, in this translation by Christopher Hampton, was first produced at the Menier Chocolate Factory on 14 September 2017. The cast was as follows:

Alice Samantha Bond
Paul Alexander Hanson
Michel Tony Gardner
Laurence Alexandra Gilbreath

Direction Lindsay Posner
Set Design Anna Fleischle
Costume Design Loren Elstein
Lighting Design Howard Harrison
Sound Design Gregory Clarke
Original Music Isobel Waller-Bridge

Le Mensonge in its original French production opened at the Théâtre Édouard-VII, Paris, on 23 September 2015, directed by Bernard Murat with Pierre Arditi and Evelyne Bouix.

Characters

Paul
Alice
Michel
Laurence

THE LIE

A living room.

In the centre, a door leading to the kitchen.
Three other doors are required: leading to
the bedroom, the dining room and the entrance hall.

The set should be as simple as possible.

The blackouts between scenes should be
as brief as possible.

One

Alice is sitting on the sofa. She's deep in thought. Perhaps even anxious. She has a glass of wine in her hand. Suddenly, Paul comes in.

Paul Ah, there you are. Are you ready? I expect they'll be here quite soon . . .

He notices that Alice is holding a glass of wine.

But . . . what are you doing?

Alice Me?

Paul Yes. You've already poured yourself a drink.

Alice (*elsewhere*) Was I not supposed to?

Paul Perhaps we should have waited for them, don't you think?

Alice The bottle was open.

Paul So it can breathe. It's a wine that needs to breathe before it can take on its full character. Anyway . . . doesn't matter. What do you think of it?

Alice Mm?

Paul I've been looking everywhere for your mother's decanter, you know, the one she offered us. The one that went with the family dinner service . . .

Brief pause.

Are you listening to me?

Alice Yes.

Paul You don't know where it is?

Alice Haven't a clue.

She drinks another mouthful. Paul is waiting for a reaction.

Paul Well?

Alice Well, what?

Paul Do you like it? The wine, I mean . . . Do you like it?

Alice Don't know.

Paul (*worried*) You don't like it?

She's not paying very much attention.

Alice Mm? Yes. It's fine.

Paul Fine . . .

Alice Yes. Isn't it?

Paul It's a good wine, you know.

Alice Is it?

Paul Yes. In fact, it's a *really* good wine.

Alice You mean it was *really* expensive?

Paul Let's just say it's a deliciously expensive wine. I've opened two bottles, but I would have preferred to decant them. That's why . . . You don't remember your mother offering us that decanter?

Alice No.

Paul Yes, you do, the decanter that went with that dinner service she gave you a couple of years ago.

Alice (*animatedly*) I just told you I don't remember. Why do you keep badgering me about this decanter?

She gets up and moves away. Brief pause.

Paul Why are you behaving like this?

Brief pause.

What is it, darling?

Brief pause.

All I was saying is it's not a house wine. It needs decanting before you serve it. That's all. I don't understand why you're getting so annoyed.

Alice I'm not getting annoyed. It's just . . .

Paul What?

Alice Actually, I need to talk to you.

Paul Oh?

Alice Yes.

Paul What's going on?

Pause.

Alice? Is there a problem?

Alice Yes.

Pause.

Paul What's the matter, darling?

Alice I'm not sure about dinner this evening . . .

Paul Not sure?

Alice No.

Paul Not sure about what?

Alice (*turning to him*) Do you think it's too late to cancel?

Paul Cancel? You mean . . . dinner?

Alice Yes.

Paul Why?

Alice I don't know. I don't feel like it.

Paul But, darling, what's the matter with you?

Alice Nothing.

Paul I mean, do you realise what you're saying? They're arriving in . . . I don't know . . . Less than half an hour . . .

Alice Exactly. So there's time to cancel.

Paul But you can't do that. At the last minute. It's not done.

Alice Michel's your friend, isn't he? He'll understand.

Paul But why do you want to cancel it? What I mean is, I mean . . . Is something wrong?

Alice No, it's just . . . I don't know. I've gone off the idea of dinner for four like that. Two couples. I've gone off it.

Paul What are you talking about? A couple of days ago, you were saying the exact opposite . . . You were complaining to me that we never had anyone for dinner.

Alice I said that?

Paul Yes. That's why . . . I thought if we invited them this evening, it'd be nice for you.

Alice I know, I know. But I have this meeting tomorrow morning . . . I have to do this presentation in front of the whole commission. And it's . . . Well, you know, it's important. I've been working on this project for weeks and weeks. And I still haven't quite got my head around it . . . Do you understand?

Paul But why are you only telling me now? I mean: at the last minute.

Alice I thought it was a good idea. That it might shake up my ideas a bit. But in the end I was mistaken. I should have opted for peace and quiet before tomorrow's meeting.

Paul You might have told me sooner, darling.

Alice I know. I'm sorry.

Paul (*worried*) This is really stupid. I've opened both bottles.

Alice We'll have dinner together.

Paul All right.

Alice Really? You only have to tell them I'm not feeling well. Or something along those lines.

Paul Very good. If that's what you want . . .

He moves reluctantly towards the telephone.

But tell me, just one thing . . .

Alice What?

Paul If you want to cancel, it's not a problem, I'll call them. But I'd just like to know . . . Is that the real reason? I mean . . . Is this meeting the reason you want to cancel?

Pause.

Tell me the truth.

Pause. She doesn't answer. She looks embarrassed.

That's what I thought. It's nothing to do with your meeting, is it?

Alice No.

Paul Then explain it to me. Has something happened?

Pause.

Paul Alice? Has something . . .?

Alice (*interrupting him*) Yes.

Paul What?

   Pause.

What happened?

Alice Nothing.

Paul Alice, this is starting to get tiring. Talk to me. You just told me something had happened. What were you referring to? And don't say 'nothing' . . .

Alice It's Michel.

Paul Sorry?

Alice I was referring to Michel.

Paul Oh?

   Pause.

Something's happened with Michel?

Alice Stop it, why are you pressuring me like this? You can see I don't want to talk about it.

Paul (*impatiently*) What happened?

Alice I'm not sure I ought to tell you.

Paul (*restraining himself*) Alice, I'm about an inch away from losing it. Let me ask you one last time and I'm asking you very calmly . . . *What happened?*

Alice I'm embarrassed to tell you. Michel is one of your best friends and . . .

Paul All the more reason! Now, what is this all about?

   Brief pause.

If you don't explain it to me, I'm not going to call them.

This argument finally seems decisive.

Alice I went shopping just now, down by the Galeries Lafayette and . . . Well, actually, not really by the Galeries Lafayette, but, you know, in behind the rue des Mathurins, if you're heading down the boulevard . . . You know, not the rue Tronchet side, the other side, yes, left of the church . . .

Paul (*impatiently*) Yes, all right, fine, you were going shopping . . . And . . . ?

Alice I was in a taxi and I passed him.

Paul Who?

Alice Michel.

Paul You passed Michel in the street?

Alice Yes. He was coming out of a shop on the rue des Mathurins, I passed right by him in the taxi.

Paul And that's why you want to cancel dinner?

Alice No. It's because, as I passed by him, he was kissing a woman. And I mean: not Laurence. Another woman.

Paul Are you joking?

Alice No.

Paul This afternoon, you saw Michel kissing another woman in the street? Is that what you're telling me?

Alice Yes.

Paul (*incredulous, almost amused*) Really, Alice . . . Think about it . . . Michel? It's not possible. Really, Alice . . . Michel? Let me remind you, Michel is my best friend!

Alice So?

Paul Mm? But he worships his wife. He's . . . He . . . In the street? Michel? No . . . I'm sure you've made a mistake. You've probably mixed him up with someone else . . .

Alice I'm telling you it was him. I absolutely recognised him.

Paul But Alice . . . *Michel?*

Alice I know.

Paul (*as if it was really improbable*) *Michel?*

Alice Yes.

Paul (*as if to himself*) *Michel?*

   Pause. He pours himself a glass of wine.

Alice Aren't you going to say anything?

Paul What do you want me to say? I'm thunderstuck.

Alice You're *what?*

Paul Thunderstuck.

Alice The word is thunderstruck, Paul.

Paul Mm?

Alice Nothing. Doesn't matter.

   Pause. Paul looks devastated.

Paul (*realising the dinner is possibly compromised*) And to think I opened both bottles . . .

Alice Has he not spoken to you about it?

Paul What?

Alice What do you think? About this girl . . . You didn't know he was . . . I mean . . . Did you know?

Paul Mm?

Alice Did you know?

Paul (*defensively*) Me?

Alice (*definite*) You did know.

Paul No, I didn't. Of course I didn't. I mean, just imagine . . . *Michel!* I'm almost as close to Laurence as I am to him. How could I have known? No, I'm flabbergasted. Literally flabbergasted.

Alice Me too. So that's why . . . the idea of having dinner with them this evening makes me really uncomfortable . . .

Paul I can see that. On the other hand, it's none of our business. I mean: it's their life. Not ours.

Alice Maybe. But I don't want to lie to Laurence.

Paul All it takes is not to say anything. Not talk about it. Maybe we don't have to cancel dinner.

Alice Really, Paul . . . It's impossible. I'm her friend.

Paul Exactly.

Alice What do you want? You want me to behave as if nothing's happened?

Paul Obviously.

Alice It's impossible.

Paul What? What's impossible? You're not planning to tell Laurence?

Pause.

You're not planning to tell her?

Alice I don't know.

Paul But you can't. You don't have the right.

Brief pause.

Alice . . .

Alice What?

Paul You're planning to tell Laurence you saw Michel with another woman?

No answer.

Why would you do a thing like that?

Alice Because she's my friend.

Paul (*trying to put things into perspective*) Your friend, your friend . . .

Alice Yes, I'm sorry. She's my friend.

Paul Before anything else, she's Michel's wife. *Michel!* And first of all, he's *my* friend.

Alice And she's my friend.

Paul Yes, but you originally met her because she was Michel's wife. Am I wrong? So, from a purely chronological point of view, she was *my* friend's wife before she was *your* friend.

Alice So? What difference does that make?

Paul Mm? It does make a difference.

Alice It makes no difference whatsoever. She's one of my friends. I'm close to her and I don't want to lie to her.

Paul But, Alice, it's *precisely* because she's your friend that you mustn't tell her. It seems completely obvious to me. I don't even understand how you can be considering it.

Alice Then we must not have the same idea of friendship.

Paul But think about it! What good would it do her to find out her husband was cheating on her? You'll just make her suffer for no good reason. That's all. You don't want to make her suffer, do you?

Alice (*as if stating the obvious*) No.

Paul Then don't say anything to her. Trust me.

Pause.

Anyway, frankly, I don't see it's any of her business.

Alice You don't see it's any of her business?

Paul No.

Alice I'm serious, Paul.

Paul Yes, I can see that, that's what's worrying me.

Pause.

Alice So it's not a problem for you?

Paul What?

Alice Now you know, now I've told you I saw him with another woman only a few hours ago, it's not a problem for you to have him for dinner with Laurence and act as if nothing had happened?

Paul No. I'm very sorry, but *no*. Michel's my friend. All right. But in my view this is about *his* life. He does whatever he likes. I'm not saying I approve of his attitude. I'm simply saying I prefer not to meddle in other people's concerns. That's all.

Alice You don't approve of his attitude, but you're not judging it very harshly.

Paul Well, Alice . . . Frankly . . . What are we talking about here? I mean, he hasn't committed a crime. Has he? Has he committed a crime?

13

Alice No.

Paul Well?

Brief pause.

From what you tell me, he's simply . . . simply kissed
another woman. It's really not . . .

The rest of the sentence goes missing.

Alice It's really not . . . what?

Paul Well, I mean . . . They've been together for years.
They love each other. That, I'm certain of. They worship
each other. All the rest is details.

Alice Is that what you think?

Paul Yes, it is . . .

Alice Perhaps you're right.

Paul Of course I am. We're not going to make a song
and dance, just because, supposedly, he's kissed another
woman . . . What's more, in the street . . . In front of
a shop.

Alice No. You're right. It happens all the time.

Paul Yes.

Alice To everyone.

Paul (*trying to play it down*) Yes, of course.

Brief pause.

Well, not to everyone. No. Obviously. But I mean: there
we are, as we know, these things can happen. *They exist.*
It's not as if this evening we're discovering for the first
time that people's emotional life is sometimes . . .

Alice Sometimes what . . . ?

Paul Chaotic. I don't know. Contradictory. Complicated. Everyone does the best he can. Don't you think?

Alice Yes. Maybe.

Paul Especially as . . .

Alice Especially as *what*?

Paul Nothing.

Alice Go on, say it . . .

Paul How can I put it? If this girl had the slightest importance to him, he'd have talked to me about her. Believe me. I'm his friend. And I didn't even know about it. So there you are.

Pause.

Come on, love . . . I completely understand it's not very comfortable for you, but let's try to be philosophical about it, shall we?

Alice Listen . . . I'm sorry. I'd really prefer to cancel . . .

Paul Fine.

Alice I'm too angry with him. I know myself, I wouldn't be able to pretend and I just don't want to put myself in that situation.

Paul All right. Just as you like.

He picks up the telephone and dials Michel's number.

I think it's a pity, but all right . . .

Alice It'll make things infinitely easier for everyone, believe me.

Paul It's your decision.

Suddenly, the bell rings. He freezes.

Alice Shit. Are they here already?

Paul I told you. They're on time.

Alice What are we going to do?

Paul Mm? What do you think we're going to do? We have no choice. We're going to open the door. But Alice . . .

Alice What?

Paul I'm trusting you. Mm? This is important. You mustn't say anything to Laurence . . . Promise me? Darling? My love? My sweetheart? Promise me?

Pause.

Alice? Promise me?

Alice No.

Pause. Blackout.

Two

Alice, Paul, Laurence and Michel are in the living room. Paul has a bottle in his hand. He's offering Michel a glass of wine.

Paul Michel?

Michel No, thanks.

Paul You don't want any?

Michel It's good of you, but no.

Paul Sure? Not even a little taste.

Michel Not even that. Thanks.

Paul (*piqued*) That's a shame. As you're such a great wine-lover.

Michel Actually, I'm not drinking, I'm trying to hold out for a month.

Paul Oh? How many days to go?

Michel Thirty. I started yesterday.

Paul Ah, yes, I see . . . It's just it's a very good wine. So it's a shame.

Michel I know. But what can you do? I have to pay attention to these things.

Laurence Michel believes he has to lose several kilos. And the world turns upside-down.

Paul I haven't had time to decant it, but I think you'll like it. Look . . . Château Lafite!

Michel No, really, it's lovely of you, but I prefer not to make any exceptions.

Paul Just as you like. Laurence, would you . . . ?

Laurence (*displaying some hesitation*) I . . . Yes, I . . . Thanks.

Alice Unless you'd prefer a glass of champagne?

Black look from Paul.

Laurence Oh, maybe I would. Would I?

Alice Would you like some champagne?

Laurence I don't want you to have to open a bottle specially for me.

Alice There's one in the fridge.

Laurence No, that's fine, a drop of wine . . .

Paul It's a very good wine recommended by my wine merchant. He's a splendid chap. Very civilised.

Michel Really?

Paul Yes. Château Lafite.

Alice We'll drink it later, Paul. With the rabbit. All right? For our aperitif, let's open the champagne. That'll be more festive. I'll go and fetch a bottle.

Laurence I'll come with you.

Laurence gets up.

Paul No, wait a minute.

Laurence What?

He doesn't want Alice and Laurence to be alone together in the kitchen.

Paul (*to Alice*) Why do you need to go together?

Alice Sorry?

Paul I'll come with you.

Alice What are you talking about? It doesn't need three of us.

Paul You're right. So you stay here, darling. Come on, Laurence . . .

Laurence No, it's all right, I'll go. Is it in the fridge?

Paul No.

Brief pause.

You're our guest. You're not to move. Alice, do you know where it is?

Alice Yes.

Paul Then would you be so good as to go and fetch it?

Alice I'm going.

Paul Thanks. That's lovely.

Alice goes out.

There we are. She'll be back in a minute.

Michel What's the matter with you, old man?

Paul Me?

Michel Yes. Are you all right? You seem a little tense.

Paul Not at all. What makes you say that? Everything's fine. On the contrary. The thing is, no, I meant to tell you . . .

He checks to see that Alice isn't able to hear him.

Well. Alice has to present her project tomorrow morning.

Laurence Tomorrow? Already?

Paul Yes. In front of the whole commission. It's an important presentation. She's been working on it for weeks and weeks.

Laurence Yes, I know.

Paul So, there we are, now you know what's going on. You understand the context. Don't hold it against her if she's a little bit, what, yes, tense this evening . . .

Alice returns.

Alice What were you saying?

Paul Me? Nothing. I was telling Laurence that . . . that she looks magnificent in that dress.

Laurence Stop it . . . No, he was telling us that you have your presentation tomorrow. You should have told us. Perhaps this dinner party's not come at a a very good time for you.

Alice No, no. Please don't worry.

A penetrating look at Paul.

Otherwise, you can be sure we'd have cancelled it.

Paul (*as if stating the obvious*) Yes.

Alice Laurence, can I pour you a glass?

Laurence I'd love one.

Paul Wait, listen, I'll do it . . .

Alice Funny, I was thinking the same thing just now. About your dress.

Laurence You were?

Alice Yes. It is magnificent!

Laurence Thank you. Michel found it for me.

Alice You go shopping now, do you?

Michel It happens. Not very often, but it happens.

Paul Laurence . . .

He hands her a glass of champagne.

Alice Whereabouts?

Michel Sorry?

Alice When you go shopping, where do you go? Galeries Lafayette? Rue des Mathurins . . . ? Not the rue Tronchet side, no, the other side, by the church . . . Somewhere like that?

Michel Not particularly. No. It depends. Why?

Alice No reason.

Paul hands Alice a glass.

Paul Here you are, darling. Michel, can I get you something? A glass of water . . . Fruit juice? Anything?

Michel Nothing, thanks. I'm fine.

Paul (*to Michel*) How are things?

Michel Good.

Laurence He never stops working.

Alice Poor thing.

Paul Published any good books lately?

Alice That reminds me, Michel, I was wondering . . . When someone hands in a really bad manuscript . . .

Michel Yes?

Alice Which must happen?

Michel Daily.

Alice What do you say to the author?

Michel I simply tell him I'm not going to publish it. Why?

Alice But if he's a friend of yours. If he's a close friend . . . Do you tell him the truth?

Paul Alice . . .

Alice What?

Paul Don't start this again.

Alice I was just wondering. It's interesting, don't you think?

Michel If he's a close friend and his book is particularly bad, I soften the blow a bit, certainly.

Paul Obviously. You can't just brutally say: 'By the way, old boy, your book is dogshit.'

Michel (*amused*) No.

Alice So you agree with Paul?

Michel What about?

Alice Paul thinks telling a lie is a sign of friendship.

Paul I didn't say that. I said that in certain cases, not telling the truth can actually be motivated by a kind impulse of a friendly nature.

Michel Yes. It's called 'tact'. Isn't it?

Paul That's it. That's the exact word. 'Tact'. Forgive me for being tactful, Alice.

Alice So you don't always tell your friends the truth?

Michel Why are you asking me these questions?

Paul (*a diversionary tactic*) Michel, are you sure you wouldn't like a glass of water or something? Or a peanut? No one's touched them. I could take it personally. So, really: no one's tempted by the peanuts?

Brief pause.

Michel What's your point?

Alice The other day I found myself in a slightly similar situation, as it happens. A kind of moral dilemma. And I thought to myself you might be able to throw some light on it. Because I have no idea what to do.

Laurence What are the circumstances?

Alice I was walking down the street, or to be absolutely precise, I was in a taxi, when I suddenly . . .

Paul Alice . . .

Alice What?

Paul Nothing. It's just they're not interested.

Alice Why do you say that?

Paul Because. They're not interested. Are you interested? See. They're not interested.

Laurence Of course we are.

Paul You're not! I mean, I take taxis! So does he! Frankly, there's nothing out of the ordinary about taking taxis. Let's change the subject. Shall we? I mean, tell me how your agency is doing, all that sort of thing. Is it going well?

Laurence Yes, thanks. But Alice was telling us something . . .

Alice *(to Paul)* Anyway, shouldn't you go and check the dinner?

Paul What dinner?

Alice What dinner do you think?

He checks his watch.

Paul No, no. It's fine.

Alice Are you sure?

Michel What are you cooking?

Laurence (*to Michel*) But Alice was in the middle of telling us something, Michel . . .

Michel Yes, sorry.

Alice Thank you, Laurence.

Paul (*to Michel*) Rabbit.

Alice gives Paul a black look, which forces him to justify himself.

I was just answering Michel's question.

Alice Anyway, I was saying . . . I was in this taxi and all of a sudden I saw the husband of one of my friends kissing another woman.

Paul (*faking incredulity*) No!

Laurence The husband of one of your friends?

Alice Yes.

Paul Well, that's what you thought. You've always been short-sighted. Maybe you made a mistake. You're always mixing people up. Not to mention the fact that every one of us is supposed to have a double somewhere. Did you not know that? It's been proved. Scientifically. Listen, the other day, someone stopped me in the street and said: 'Hello, Patrick, how are you doing?'

Everyone is looking at Paul, amazed by his outburst. Pause.

Laurence And then?

Alice I just came upon him with this girl.

Laurence But he didn't see you.

Alice No. I passed by in a taxi and he didn't see me. But I saw him. I recognised him. Right away I called my friend to find out, you know, how she was, and I realised she had no idea what was going on.

Laurence Poor thing.

Michel And you were wondering if you ought to tell her what you'd seen?

Alice That's right.

Laurence Who was it? Do I know her?

Alice Mm?

Laurence Don't tell me it was Sylvie!

Paul Yes, it was.

Laurence It was Sylvie? I knew she hadn't been getting on with Matthieu.

Alice No, no, it wasn't Sylvie.

Paul It was, it was Sylvie!

Alice I've just said it wasn't.

Paul Wasn't it? I thought it was. Wasn't it Sylvie? Oh. That's what I thought. My mistake.

Laurence So who was it? Do I know her?

Brief pause.

Go on, you can tell me . . .

Paul No, you don't know her. She's a friend . . . a friend of the family. On my mother's side. By marriage. I mean, it's one of our friends you don't know.

Alice Anyway, she has no idea her husband is cheating on her. And I'm wondering what I ought to do.

Paul What a question! You mustn't say anything to her! You'd just cause her a lot of pointless suffering . . .

Alice We know what you think, Paul.

Paul And you're not interested, yes, I know. But all the same, I would like to add, even if, I'm prepared to concede, my opinion is of very little interest, I would just like to add that this could well be a completely trivial incident! Who knows? And by talking to your friend . . .

He inadvertently indicates Laurence, then corrects himself.

I mean the friend you were describing to us just now, whom neither of you know . . . You're taking the risk of setting off a crisis in their marriage! If that happens, you'll be resposible for their separation! Think about that, Alice! It'll be your fault!

Michel Why are you getting so upset?

Paul Mm? No, I'm not getting upset. I'm just saying if you let things go, this man . . .

Same thing: he indicates Michel, then corrects himself.

I mean: the husband of this friend neither of you know and I don't either. I don't know him! Anyway, this man will realise of his own accord that his life depends on staying with his wife. That's it. All I'm saying is that we're in agreement. I'm in favour of *tact*.

Alice (*to Laurence*) What about you, what do you think?

Laurence I don't know. It's tricky.

Alice (*sincerely*) You see, she's someone I love. And I can't work out what's the fairest and most respectful decision to make on her behalf.

Laurence I understand.

At this stage of the play, we ought not to suspect that Alice has any other motive. This is not a woman who can't bear lies and would like to tell the truth come what may. This is a woman who's fond of her friend and finds herself confronted with a moral dilemma which seems important to her: would it be more respectful to tell her the truth or to keep quiet?

Alice You, for example, would you prefer not to know anything?

Laurence Me?

Alice Yes.

Laurence You mean: if someone caught Michel with another woman?

Alice For example.

Paul A highly unlikely example, but fine.

Laurence I've never thought about it.

Brief pause. Laurence seems to be considering the question. Paul is tense. He's holding his breath.

I don't think I'd like it at all if someone took it upon themselves to tell me about it . . .

Paul (*relieved*) Hoo!

Laurence No. I'd rather not know anything than have some outsider interfering in my private life.

Paul There you are. You agree with me. Ah . . .

Laurence Some things it's best to know nothing about, don't you think?

Paul I certainly do.

Laurence I'm thinking there's a certain wisdom in accepting that you can't know *everything*.

Paul Great wisdom, you might say. Very great wisdom.

Alice So you'd prefer to know nothing?

Paul She's just told you she would.

Laurence Best would be that something like that never happened.

Alice Obviously.

Laurence But I don't have too many worries on that score.

Pause. Michel takes her hand.

Paul (*aiming to change the subject*) Great. Shall we talk about something else? Yes? You never told me . . . how things are going at the agency.

Laurence Mm?

Paul Things improving?

Laurence I wouldn't go so far as to say that . . . Ever since Simone retired, I've been landed with twice as much work. The week never seems to end. I'm worn out.

Alice You don't look it.

Laurence That's nice of you.

Alice No, it's true. I was looking at you just now and I thought to myself, on the contrary, you're gorgeous. Really gorgeous. Don't you think, Michel?

Michel What, that . . . ?

Alice That Laurence is gorgeous.

Laurence (*trying to brush off the compliment*) Oh, come on . . .

Michel I have to confess I've always had a slight weakness for my wife.

Paul Me too.

Brief pause.

I mean, for mine.

Laurence Otherwise, everything's all right. I'm going to Quiberon for a few days next week to lie down.

Alice On your own?

Laurence Yes. Perfect, don't you think? Can you imagine? Spot of hydrotherapy. It's exactly what I need.

Alice (*to Michel*) Aren't you tempted to go too?

Michel I'd have loved to. But I have too much work.

Alice Of course. Poor thing. What are you going to do all alone in Paris without your wife?

Laurence Don't worry about him. He manages very well without me.

Alice Oh, no, I'm not worrying.

Paul Anyone care for a peanut?

Pause. Alice exhales. How can Laurence not understand?

Laurence (*to Alice*) What's the matter?

Alice Me?

Laurence Yes. You seem gloomy . . .

Alice No, not at all. I . . . I was just thinking about what we were saying.

Laurence When?

Alice Just now. I was thinking maybe you were right, there probably is a kind of wisdom in accepting the fact that there are certain things you can't know . . .

Laurence I think so, don't you?

Paul No, I don't believe this! You're not going to start on all that again? We were talking about Quiberon. We were talking about Brittany!

Laurence For example, if I was to surprise Paul with another woman one day . . .

Paul Here we go, off again!

Laurence If I've understood you correctly, you would want me to come and tell you.

Alice Yes.

Laurence I'd never do that.

Alice Why?

Laurence I don't know. You're my friends. I wouldn't want to cause a row between you.

Paul In any case, it's not something that will ever happen. So let's change the subject.

Laurence You never know.

Paul Of course you do. You want me to tell you why? Because, even if sometimes she can be really irritating, I'm completely crazy about my wife.

Michel Me too.

   Brief pause.

I mean about mine, obviously.

   Paul and Laurence laugh. Pause.

The basic problem, Alice, is that whatever they may claim, people don't really want to be told the truth.

Alice Is that what you think?

Michel I know from experience. When I started out, you can't imagine how many writers I infuriated because I made the mistake of telling them honestly what I thought of their manuscripts . . . In the end, every one of them resented me. And I'm prepared to bet this friend of yours, the one you were telling us about, would wind up holding it against you, if you told her what you saw.

Alice So lying's the only answer?

Michel Let's say, keeping your secrets.

Alice (*coldly*) Right. I'm going to check the dinner.

She gets up abruptly.

Paul No, don't worry, I'll do it.

Alice No, no. That's all right.

She goes out. Her departure leaves a chill behind.

Michel What's the matter with her?

Paul I don't know.

Michel Did I say something?

Paul No, no, I don't think so. She's just gone to check the dinner, you know, the what-d'you-call-it, the rabbit.

Laurence I'll go and see if she needs a hand.

Paul No! No, not you.

Laurence What?

Michel All right. I'll go. I somehow think it'd be better if I go . . . Don't you think?

Paul Yes. Maybe.

Michel Let me try and put things right . . . But d'you think it's to do with what I just said?

Paul No. I don't think so.

Michel Fine. I'll go and see. I'll be back.

He goes out.

Laurence What's the matter with her?

Paul She's a bit stressed because of her meeting tomorrow.

Laurence No, seriously . . . Is something going on?

Pause.

What's going on?

Blackout.

Three

A little later in the evening. Alice is on the sofa, as Paul closes the door on the guests.

Paul Goodbye. Goodbye . . . And thanks again . . . Yes, yes. Safe trip. Safe trip.

The door closes. He turns towards Alice. Long pause. He moves back into the living room.

I expect you're relieved.

Alice Very.

Paul Well, that's something.

Alice I loathed that dinner party.

Paul Yes, I think you made that clear to everyone.

Pause. He pours himself another glass of wine.

Well, you realise what you've done?

Alice Me?

Paul Yes. You were unbearable from start to finish.

Alice I told you I didn't feel like it.

Paul That's no excuse.

Alice All you had to do was cancel it, like I asked you to.

Paul Yes, I remember you asked me to. Ten minutes before they arrived.

Pause.

You can't behave like that, darling. These people are our friends. Or at any rate, they're people I like very much. I don't know if you realise how hateful you were to Michel.

Alice You're exaggerating.

Paul Not in the least. You were aggressive, you kept making really double-edged remarks, you even walked out of the room for no reason.

Alice I went to check the rabbit because you were refusing to go.

Paul No, you left the room quite brutally, to demonstrate your opposition to what was being said. I was dreadfully embarrassed. Really, it's not the way to behave.

Alice Well, did you see the way he was making up to Laurence?

Paul Who? Michel?

Alice Yes. What a bastard! Did you see him? He never stopped kissing her and being lovey-dovey and deferring to her and flattering her . . .

Paul Shocking.

Alice You don't understand.

Paul What?

Brief pause.

What don't I understand?

Alice I don't know. That dinner party was one of the most abject occasions I've ever attended in my life.

Paul And I'm the one who's exaggerating . . .

Alice It's true.

Paul Still no reason to be so unpleasant.

Pause. As if she's regretting her behaviour, she now tries to be nice to him.

Alice Any left?

Paul Any what?

Alice Wine . . . Could you pour me a glass?

He does so.

Thanks.

Pause. Alice tries to cheer him up.

It's very good, anyway.

Paul (*still a bit annoyed*) It's Château Lafite. So of course it is.

Pause. Her manner is softer. It's clear she wants to be forgiven.

Alice You really think I behaved badly?

Paul Yes.

Alice I was that hateful?

Pause.

I don't know why I take these things to heart so much. But I've always been like that. Since I was little. I can't bear lying. It makes me go on the attack . . .

Pause.

Are you angry with me?

Pause. He remains inscrutable.

I'm sorry, Paul.

Pause.

I'll phone Laurence in the morning to apologise, tell her I wasn't feeling very well. That I was in a funny mood. I'll think of something.

Paul Yes, that would be good.

Alice I'll phone her in the morning. All right? But please don't be angry with me.

Pause.

Come on . . . please . . .

A sense of calm returns. She makes a loving gesture.

Paul But you know, you're probably being so hard on him because you don't know the whole story . . . You mustn't think it's necessarily that easy for him.

Alice What are you talking about?

Paul This business. It just fell on top of him. He could have happily done without it. Believe me.

Alice You're talking about what? This girl?

Paul Yes.

Alice What makes you say that?

Paul He told me.

Pause. He realises he shouldn't have said this.

Alice What?

Paul Mm?

Alice What did you say?

Paul Me?

Alice Michel told you?

Paul Not really, he . . .

Alice So you knew about it?

Paul (*on the defensive*) Me?

Alice You knew about it.

Paul No.

Alice Yes. You just said. Did he talk to you about it? Obviously he talked to you about it! You're his best friend. Did he talk to you about it, yes or no?

Paul Well, yes, he vaguely referred to it, yes, well . . .

Alice In other words, you knew.

Paul More or less. I didn't know it was still going on.

Alice You mean it's been going on for some time?

Paul Mm? Listen, Alice, we don't have to go into detail.

Alice Why did you tell me you didn't know about it?

Paul Alice, please. Let's talk about something else. Shall we? Would you like another glass? Unless you'd rather go to bed? Might be a better idea, don't you think, you have that meeting in the morning. What time is it? Yes, it's late, look. I'm exhausted. Aren't you?

Brief pause.

Alice (*darkly*) He told you.

Paul He made some vague reference to it once. Yes . . . Very vague.

Alice When?

Paul I don't know, I can't remember. What's it matter? Alice . . .

She's moving away.

Well, all right, it's true, I did know about it. There we are. Happy? I've no idea *who* this girl is, but he's talked to me about her several times. She's done his head in.

37

What can I tell you? I completely understand that you were uncomfortable this evening and I'm really sorry. But, you know, it's nothing to do with me and it's late and you're tired. And you have your meeting tomorrow. And . . .

Alice Why do you say she's done his head in?

Paul That's what he told me.

Alice Has he known her long?

Paul I don't know. All I know is the situation's been very difficult for him . . .

Alice Poor thing . . .

Paul Why be sarcastic? What do you know about the details of this business?

Alice Much less than you do, apparently.

Paul Right, well, now you know. It's been very hard for him. He's been through the mill. It's been like an infatuation. But Laurence is the woman in his life. He knows that. He loves her.

Alice He loves her and he lies to her.

Paul That's right . . . It's not necessarily a contradiction.

Alice Isn't it?

Paul No. Sometimes it's harder to lie, Alice. To keep all that inside. Believe me.

Alice How would you know?

Paul Mm?

Alice How would you know?

Paul Mm? Well, I . . . no. All I'm saying is that sometimes lying is a sign of love. As opposed to what you're saying. That's all I'm saying.

38

Alice Lying is a sign of love?

Paul Yes. *Sometimes.*

Alice I thought it was a sign of friendship.

Paul It can also be a sign of love.

Alice Ah, it works for love as well? It's versatile.

Paul (*as if he's uttering some deep thought*) Not always, Alice. Not always.

Brief pause.

Alice Can I ask you a question? And I want a really sincere answer . . .

Paul What?

Alice Are you saying this to defend your friend or is that really what you think?

Paul (*beseechingly*) Alice . . . What is it you're after? I can't even understand why we're arguing about this.

Alice We're not arguing. We're having a discussion.

Paul Then let's discuss something else. This is starting to get really tiresome.

Pause. She moves away from him a bit.

What?

Alice Nothing. I'm trying to imagine you, that's all.

Paul Who?

Alice The two of you. You and Michel. I'm trying to imagine your conversations. Your little man secrets . . . You disgust me.

Paul What's this 'you'? What does any of this have to do with me? I am in no way complicit with this sort of thing, Alice.

Alice You're not?

Paul No. In no way.

Alice 'I'm thunderstuck.'

Paul Sorry?

Alice 'I'm thunderstuck.' Isn't that what you said to me just now, when I told you I'd seen Michel kissing another woman? You pretended you couldn't get over it, you said you were 'flabbergasted', when you knew perfectly well all along.

Paul Yes, all right . . .

Alice You know very well you are complicit and I find that disgusting. For her sake as well as for mine.

Paul Darling . . .

Alice (*almost to herself*) Things would be so much simpler if everyone told the truth . . .

Paul It'd be a real nightmare, Alice. If everyone told the truth, there wouldn't be a single couple left on earth.

Alice There wouldn't be a single couple left on earth?

Paul (*as if it were self-evident*) No.

Brief pause. He corrects himself.

I mean, it's just an expression.

Alice Can you expand? I'm interested.

Paul Oh, sweetheart . . . No, please . . . Don't start. All I'm saying is that in certain situations, a lie is a way of sparing other people.

Alice Delighted to find out.

Paul You don't believe me? You want an example? Is that it? All right. Let's take the case of this evening.

Suppose everyone had told the truth . . . Just suppose . . . Can you imagine the carnage? You'd have told Laurence her husband was cheating on her. Great! Wonderful! We would have achieved a small marital crisis; always, whatever anyone says, extremely entertaining! Then I'd have told Michel that he's undoubtedly a very good editor but that his own novels are unreadable. It's true, and he's my friend, he deserves the truth! He'd definitely never speak to me again, but at least I would have been honest! My conscience would be clear! I imagine after your revelations, he'd never speak to you again either. So, if you agree, we could sum up the situation as follows: if we'd told each other the truth this evening, Alice, if we'd done that, Michel would never speak to *me* again, he'd never speak to *you* again and his wife would never speak to *him* again. Wonderful! What a friendly occasion! All I'm saying is it would have been pretty hard to find a topic of conversation at dinner.

He's rather satisfied with his example.

Alice And what about us?

Paul Mm?

Alice What about us?

Paul What do you mean, *us*?

Alice I mean, us. What would happen if we told each other the truth?

Paul We do tell each other the truth, darling.

Alice I thought there wasn't a 'single couple on earth' . . .

Paul Yes, well . . .

Alice That's what you said.

Paul Clumsy expression.

Alice So you mean _we_ do tell each other the truth?

Paul Of course, darling, of course we do. I mean, darling . . . of course. What can you be thinking? Alice. Really, darling. Of course . . . The very idea!

Pause. She pours herself another glass of wine. He realises she's not going to let go of the subject.

Really, what? You pass one of my friends in the street with another woman. It's nothing to do with me, is it? Why are you attacking me? There's no sense to it! Alice! What does this mean? I love you. You know that. I'm deeply in love with you. So, please, darling, no more of this sort of conversation.

Alice You can understand it's a bit unsettling for me.

Paul What is?

Alice To hear you say that in the end lying is a good thing . . .

Paul (_trying to put things in perspective_) A good thing, a good thing . . . That's not exactly what I said.

Alice Isn't it?

Paul No. Not exactly. You're twisting my words!

Alice It's as if you're openly admitting to me that you don't tell me the truth.

Paul Not at all!

Alice You've been explaining to me for ten minutes that a lie is a sign of love!

Paul Not for me. Not for us.

Alice For who then? Other people?

Paul Yes, yes.

Pause. She seems annoyed.

Alice I want some reassurance . . . I do, because you're starting to make me doubt everything . . . You're saying you don't lie to me?

Paul Mm?

Alice You don't lie to me?

Paul Me?

Alice Yes. You.

Paul But, darling . . .

Alice Answer the question.

Paul No, no. Of course not.

Alice Never?

Paul No, no. Never. Of course not. Never!

Pause.

Alice This is horrible.

Paul What is?

Alice I can't manage to believe you.

Paul That's it! That's it! No, I just knew this discussion was going to lead us up shit creek . . . I knew it! Why can't you believe me?

Alice Why do you think?

Paul But I always tell you the truth. I have nothing whatsoever to hide.

Alice 'I'm thunderstuck.'

Paul Oh, do give up . . .

Alice It's the proof that you don't always tell me the truth.

Paul I was being discreet. I didn't want to make a spectacle of Michel's private life. I mean, put yourself in my place . . . He's my friend. Shit. And you're his wife's friend.

Alice What about you?

Paul What?

Alice You've never cheated on me?

Paul Mm?

Alice No, I'd like to know.

Paul What are you talking about?

Alice Tell me.

Paul Have you gone completely off your head, dearest?

Alice I'm just asking you a question. You've never cheated on me?

Paul Of course not! Never! I mean, think about it!

Alice Not even once?

Paul Really, Alice! Can you hear yourself? Can you hear yourself?

Alice Why are you reacting like this?

Paul Why do you think?

Alice After everything you've said to me this evening, it seems to me a perfectly normal question to ask.

Paul You think that's perfectly normal? Funny, because I find it quite insulting.

Alice Insulting?

Paul Absolutely. Insulting.

He pours himself another glass of wine, indignant.
Tense silence. He turns his back to her.

Alice (*conciliatory*) Paul . . . Come on . . .

Paul What?

Alice Don't close up like this.

Paul I'm not closed up.

Alice Yes, you are, you are closed up. I know you.

Paul I'm hurt. It's different.

Alice Hurt?

Paul Yes. By your insinuations.

Alice (*gently*) I'm not insinuating anything. I just asked you a question.

Paul Yes. And I answered.

Pause.

Alice There's no reason to react like this.

Pause.

You really are sensitive, Paul.

Paul Before we know where we are, this'll be my fault.

Long pause.

Alice (*back-pedalling*) All right, fine, I'm sorry. Do you forgive me?

Pause.

Paul, I'm speaking to you . . .

Pause.

Do you forgive me?

Paul (*almost grudgingly*) Yes.

Alice I'm really sorry if I hurt your feelings. I didn't mean to.

Paul I can't understand how we've finished up arguing about this. Laurence and Michel may be having marital problems, but that's no reason for us to be dragged along in their wake.

Alice You're right.

She sits down, speaks calmly and confidently.

Bur I meant it just now, you know, when I said I found that dinner party horribly sad. I don't know . . . It represented everything in life I'm most afraid of.

Pause.

Love ought to be something pure, oughtn't it? I mean: to love somebody is to be true. It's having nothing to hide. Don't you think?

Paul Yes. Of course.

Alice That's why.

Paul That's why *what*?

Alice That's why I want us to tell each other the truth.

Paul Us?

Alice Both of us.

Paul (*anxious*) But what about?

Alice What do you think?

Brief pause. She speaks gently to him. Nothing allows him to guess that a trap is being set. Right now, she's not a manipulator. She simply wants the discussion to be as honest as possible.

46

You know, for some time now, I've had the impression you've been hiding things from me.

Paul Me? Not at all! What are you going to think of next?

Alice As you see, I'm speaking to you very calmly. I just want to get to a place where we can say things to one another . . .

Paul What sort of things?

Alice I'd like you to tell me if you've ever cheated on me.

Paul I can't believe it! This is becoming a genuine obsession!

Alice Answer me.

Paul I already have.

Alice Why can't you give me a simple answer?

Paul But, darling . . .

Alice I promise I won't get angry. We've been together for years. I completely understand you must have been tempted . . . I'm not going to make a song and dance about it . . . That's not what's important to me. What's important is what we saw this evening. Two people no longer telling each other the truth.

Pause.

Do you understand what I'm saying?

Paul Yes, but . . . No, I'm just a bit surprised.

Alice Surprised?

Paul A bit, yes.

Alice Just now, you said yourself that Michel's situation was quite banal and that you refused to judge him too harshly.

47

Paul Yes.

Alice Well there you are, this is the same thing. I have no desire to judge you harshly.

Paul (*energetically*) But it's not at all the same thing! I didn't come out of a shop this afternoon and kiss a woman!

Alice Has that never happened to you?

Paul Mm?

Paul Coming out of a shop?

Alice Or anywhere.

Paul No, it hasn't!

Alice You see, I don't trust you.

Paul But I'm not going to confess to something that didn't happen just to make you feel good!

Alice So, it's never happened to you?

Paul No! But you realise what it is we're saying to each other here? You realise the direction this conversation is heading in?

Alice We're talking honestly, that's all. There's no reason to get annoyed.

Paul I am not getting annoyed! It's just I don't see the point of this conversation.

Alice What are you afraid of?

Paul I'm not afraid. I've no reason to be afraid.

Alice Then tell me the truth.

Pause.

Since we've been together, you've never had an affair with anyone?

Pause.

48

We can talk about it, you know. We can even laugh about it. All this sort of thing isn't necessarily that important. Don't you think? Since we love one another.

Pause.

Come on . . . tell me. Surely it's happened to you once?

Pause. He's obviously tempted.

You prefer, what, to be like Laurence and Michel? Couldn't you feel the way everything sounded false this evening?

Pause.

Why are you looking at me as if I'm leading you into a trap?

Paul I don't understand why you're asking me all these questions.

Alice (*convincingly*) I need to be able to trust you again. It's quite simple. To feel we're able to tell each other the truth. No deceptions. That we're not like them. That we still love each other.

Paul I really don't see the point of . . .

Alice (*interrupting him*) Please. I'm asking you to do me this favour. I'm asking it as a sign of your love.

Brief pause.

Paul Very well.

Brief pause.

You really want to know?

Alice Yes.

Paul All right. I really don't see the point of it, but since it seems important for you to know, all right then, yes, it has happened to me. Once.

Brief pause.

Happy?

Long pause. He glances anxiously at her.

Alice (*gently*) Was it a long time ago?

Paul Mm? I don't know. Some time ago.

He's already regretting having made this confession.

Alice How did it happen?

Paul Alice . . .

Alice No, tell me.

Paul What's the point? It's all in the past.

Alice Absolutely.

Paul You wanted me to tell you the truth. I've told you. Now can we change the subject?

Alice Absolutely not, we can't. I need you to explain it to me.

Paul Explain what?

Alice What happened.

Pause.

Tell me.

Paul I've forgotten.

Alice Stop it. Tell me who it was at least. Do I know her?

Paul No.

Pause.

Alice Paul . . .

Paul What?

Alice Why are you so closed up?

Paul Because I have nothing to say.

Alice But you can see how calm I am. You have nothing to fear. Do I seem angry with you?

Pause.

Well?

Paul She was a woman I met. Just like that. It was completely unimportant.

Alice When?

Paul It happened, I don't know . . . Last summer.

She's visibly shaken.

That's when it happened. One evening, I found myself with this girl and . . . it just sort of happened. There we are.

Alice It just sort of happened?

Paul Yes.

Alice You mean, all of a sudden, you found yourself in her bed?

Paul Alice, please . . .

Alice What?

Paul What's the purpose of all these questions?

Alice To understand.

Paul There's nothing to understand. I'm telling you, it happened to me once. It had no significance. I quickly realised I wasn't that sort of man. And that was that. And I love you. You have no idea how much I love you.

He moves over to her.

Alice Leave me alone.

Paul Alice . . .

Alice How long did it last?

Paul I told you, hardly any time.

Alice Tell me . . .

Paul I can't remember.

Alice And when you went to Antibes, supposedly for your work, in March, you remember? We had a quarrel because I was sure you were going down there to be with someone . . . Was it with her?

Pause. He doesn't deny it.

Obviously it was with her.

Paul (*embarrassed*) It's more complicated than that . . .

Alice What? So, it was with her! It was in March! You know how many months there are, as a rule, between the summer and the month of March? The best part of nine months!

Paul You see, it wasn't a good idea to talk about this. You're starting to get aggressive!

Alice No, but do you realise what it is you're saying to me? Do you realise? This isn't just some little adventure! This is a total double life!

Paul No, it isn't.

Alice Yes, it is! You've been lying to me for months! If I understand correctly, you've been sleeping with this whore for months!

Paul Alice . . .

She sets off for the bedroom. He makes a vague attempt to hold her back.

What are you doing?

Alice Stop it! Don't touch me!

Paul Wait a minute . . .

Alice I'm leaving you, Paul.

Paul What?

Alice I'm leaving you.

Paul But . . .

Alice Let me through.

Paul But listen . . .

Alice I don't want to hear any more. Goodnight.

Paul But you were the one who was insisting on . . .

Alice I don't want to talk to you any more. I don't want to see you any more.

Paul What are you doing?

She goes into the bedroom and closes the door behind her.

Alice! Open the door! Alice? Listen to me. This is completely idiotic. Alice? Open the door. Darling? You can't do this to me . . . Alice . . . You push me to talk and then . . . Alice? If you knew how much I love you. I've never stopped loving you for a single mimute . . . Why are you behaving like this? Please . . . Open the door. Open the door, darling . . . Darling . . .

Pause. To himself:

I knew this discussion was taking us up shit creek. I knew it . . .

Pause. He tries to think of something to say.

Alice . . . Darling? Surely you didn't believe me, did you?

Blackout.

Four

The next morning. The sofa is in disarray and Paul's hair is all over the place. It's clear he's slept in the living room. Suddenly, the bedroom door opens, Paul stands up. Alice appears. She's dressed, already prepared to leave and go and present her project.

Paul Sweetheart . . .

Pause. She moves forward.

Sleep well?

Alice What do you think?

Paul I've made some coffee. Would you like some? I'll fetch you a cup.

Alice (*closed off*) I'm late.

Paul Have some coffee before you go to your meeting. It's important.

Pause. Paul offers her a cup of coffee.

Here you are.

Pause.

Darling, I have to talk to you.

Alice (*closed off*) I have to go.

Paul I know, but I can't spend all day in this state. It's impossible. I'm absolutely . . . We have to talk. I know you have to go, but I'm only asking for two minutes of your time. Two minutes . . .

Alice What for?

Paul If you knew . . . I'm dreadfully sorry about the way things worked out last night. I haven't slept all night. I've been stupid and I want you to forgive me. I don't know what came over me . . . You kept insisting you wanted a confession from me, so, I have no idea why, I said the first thing that came into my head and made up that improbable story . . .

Alice (*ironically*) Oh, so that's it . . .

Paul Yes. I hope you didn't believe me. You didn't believe me, did you? Did you believe me? No, because it's not true, Alice. I never had an affair with that girl.

Alice You really expect I'm going to believe you?

Paul I can see that appearances are against me, but at least let me explain . . . You asked all those questions so insistently . . . It was no good my saying I'd never cheated on you, you wouldn't have believed me and you'd just have started in again. You said I'd have to confess something to you before you'd be able to trust me again. Isn't that what you said? You asked me to as 'a sign of my love' . . . So, all right, I, after a minute, I told you what you wanted to hear. That's all. But it wasn't true.

She makes an impatient gesture.

Alice, I swear to you that I'm telling the truth! I never had an affair with that girl. Or any other girl. I said it to . . . What? I said it to make you jealous. But none of it was true. I mean, surely you can understand that if it was true, I wouldn't have told you that way.

Alice You'd have lied to me?

Paul Of course. I'm not a complete idiot.

Alice's expression indicates she may want to differ on this point.

55

Alice, please . . . I just wanted to demonstrate that this kind of conversation leads directly to fisticuffs. And you can see I was right. Look what's happened . . . I had to sleep on the sofa! Which proves I was right when I said Michel would have been wrong to tell Laurence the truth. And vice versa. That he was right to lie to her. See? I just wanted to prove it to you.

Alice You've had all night on the sofa to think about it and this is the best you could come up with?

Paul Alice, I swear to you I'm telling the truth: nothing I said was true!

She smiles, even though she's still quite upset.

What? Why are you smiling?

Alice No reason. So, if I understand what you're saying, last summer, contrary to what you were telling me last night, you did not meet this woman?

Paul Not once.

Alice And in the subsequent months, you did not have an affair with this same woman?

Paul Of course not! Really, think about it . . . Who do you take me for? After twenty years of marriage, honestly . . .

Alice And this winter, when you had to go to a conference in Antibes, it wasn't her you were going there to be with?

Paul I've never cheated on you, Alice. Never. Not in Paris, not in Antibes. Not even in Dijon, if you want to go into detail! I realise I was clumsy last night, inventing that fantastical story . . . I realise how stupid I was . . . But there we are, I felt as if I were under police interrogation and I said the first thing that came into my head!

Alice And this morning, you would like to change your statement?

Paul Exactly.

Brief pause.

Alice Listen, Paul, there's no point wearing yourself out. I don't believe you. And I have to go.

Paul (*trying to hold her back*) Listen, so, all right! All right! I'm going to tell you exactly what happened. Is that what you want? All right! Since you insist. The woman I was talking to you about, I did in fact meet her last summer.

Alice You see.

Paul Yes. I know. And if you want to know, I even had dinner with her . . .

Alice Paul . . .

Paul You don't believe me? I had dinner with her, I remember this, it was . . . in a restaurant. There we are. Now you know everything. And please note that I will not conceal from you the fact that, yes, I got into a taxi with her.

Alice But, naturally, you dropped her at her place . . .

Paul Mm? No.

He's caught on the hop, since in fact that was what he was going to say.

She suggested I have a drink with her at her place, you understand what I'm saying. I'm trying to be transparent, but . . .

Alice But you refused.

Paul Mm? No, I . . . accepted. I admit it. I completely understood the implications of this sort of suggestion, and yet, and you see, I'm telling you about it, I accepted. But once I got up there . . .

Alice You didn't feel well.

Paul Something like that, yes. Because I started thinking about you and how much I love you and even if I might have been tempted for a moment, I realised I didn't really feel capable of going through with it. I got frightened and I left.

She shakes her head.

If I'm telling you all this, it's so that you'll know the truth. And forgive me.

Alice Forgive you what? Since nothing happened with this woman.

Paul Mm?

Alice You'd like me to forgive you for what, exactly?

Paul Mm? For last night's lie. I played with fire and I shouldn't have.

She shakes her head as if to say: 'How can you expect me to swallow a routine like that?'

You find it incredible? Is that it? I agree with you. It's impossible to believe . . . Which is what proves I'm telling the truth.

Alice Oh, yes?

Paul Yes. If I'd been lying, I'd have told you something believable. Unassailable. Don't you think? That's what liars do. Apparently. Whereas, let's be honest, my story doesn't stand up. You agree?

Alice Yes.

Paul This story about going up to the girl's place and then leaving immediately, it reeks of lies! Who'd ever swallow a routine like that? Nobody! No. I hate to say it, but it isn't believable! That's what proves it's the truth.

Alice You really think I'm an idiot or what?

Paul Not at all.

Alice In any case, it's a grotesque situation. And it's really more up to me to ask for forgiveness.

Paul You?

Alice Yes.

Paul Why?

Alice I shouldn't have reacted like that. After all, I'm the one who pushed you to speak. I even begged you to. I had no right to react so violently afterwards . . .

Paul Well, I must say . . .

Alice But at that moment, you see, something inside me crumbled.

Paul I understand, darling. And I'm really sorry.

Alice Me too. Really. I shouldn't have reacted so violently.

Paul (*thinking reconciliation is on the cards*) Come on . . .

Alice Especially as . . .

Paul As what?

Alice No, I have to go, Paul. I don't want to be late. We'll talk about it this evening.

Paul What was it you wanted to say?

Alice Nothing. I just wanted you to know . . . I wasn't setting a trap for you last night, when I said we had to get to a place where we could tell each other the truth.

Paul I know, sweetheart.

Alice But when you brought up that relationship . . . I don't know . . . I was suddenly overwhelmed by an

59

irrational anger . . . All the more irrational and unfair, because it's something that had also happened to me.

Paul I know, darling.

Brief pause.

What?

Alice To some extent, I think that's why I embarked on that conversation last night, to tell you.

Paul Tell me what? What are you talking about?

Alice I only hope you won't hold it against me, my volcanic reaction. And making you sleep on the sofa.

Paul Of course not, darling. Of course not. No, but, there's just one thing, I'm not sure I understood correctly. What also happened to you?

Alice Having an affair.

Paul Sorry?

Alice I thought about it all night. And I told myself I couldn't demand the truth from you, if I was hiding things on my side.

Paul Mm? What is all this? Are you telling me you've been cheating on me? Is that what you're telling me, Alice?

Alice Don't get angry, please.

Paul What? But . . . What? Is that it? Alice, are you joking? Are you pulling my leg? Aren't you?

Brief pause.

You've had an affair . . . You mean with *another man*?

Suddenly, he's very disturbed.

But when? How? What is all this?

Alice What's it matter? It's all in the past.

Paul Are you joking? Are you joking?

Pause.

(*Positive.*) You're joking.

Alice No.

Paul I don't believe you.

Alice All right. Don't believe me. What do you want me to tell you?

Paul The truth.

Alice I've just told you.

Pause. He sits down.

Anyway, I have to go. I'm already late.

Paul (*getting up again*) Mm? You're crazy, Alice. Are you crazy? You're staying here.

Alice We'll talk about it this evening. You know very well this is a very important meeting. I can't allow myself to be late.

Paul Listen, do you realise what you just said to me? Do you realise? You want to go off to work as if nothing's happened, when you've just told me you've had an affair? And with another man!

Alice Calm down.

Paul You want me to calm down? First of all, what is all this? When did it start? Who was it? Alice, who was it? When did it start, this business?

Alice Doesn't matter. 'It just sort of happened.' That's all.

Paul (*recognising the quotation*) I don't believe you. You're just saying it to make me feel jealous. You're saying it to get revenge.

Alice Think what you like. In any case, I have to go.

Paul You're staying here, Alice! I mean, what, you want to drive me crazy?

Alice Paul, please . . . It's not as if this morning we're discovering that people's emotional life is sometimes . . . 'Chaotic. I don't know. Contradictory. Complicated.'

Paul Will you stop taking the piss? I can't stand it when people are taking the piss.

Alice (*darkly*) Neither can I.

Pause.

Paul Are you seriously telling me you've had an affair . . .? Is it true?

Alice Yes.

Paul You're lying.

Alice All right. Just as you like. Now will you let me go.

Paul You can't leave me like this! You can't do that to me!

Alice puts her coat on.

But who was it? Alice! Just tell me that. Just tell me . . . Do I know him? Who is it? Is it . . .? Who is it, Alice? Who is it?

Alice Who do you think?

She smiles at him. Then she leaves. Pause. Blackout.

Five

Paul and Michel.

Michel And you have no idea who it might be?

Paul None whatsoever. I spent all morning imagining various possibilities, but I got nowhere. It's driving me insane.

Michel You oughtn't to let yourself get in this state.

Paul I know, but I can't help it. I'm in the most terrible pain.

Michel Poor old sod.

Pause.

Paul Any case, it's really nice of you to come round.

Michel No big deal. That's what friends are for.

Paul Yes.

Michel I could tell on the phone you were in a bad way.

Paul I must have called her a dozen times, but she hasn't called back.

Michel She had her meeting this morning! You wouldn't expect her to answer.

Paul I know.

Michel So?

Pause.

Paul No. I thought it might be Hervon. You know, the architect . . .

Michel The old guy?

Paul Yes, you agree, not too plausible . . .

Michel No.

Paul Yes, that's what I told myself. I know she adores him . . . So I thought . . . But no, you're right, it's not plausible. She wouldn't sleep with a man like that.

Michel Anyway, what's it matter?

Paul What's what matter? Knowing who it is?

Michel Yes. What difference does it make to you? She said it was all over. Didn't she? So?

Paul She said nothing.

Michel Oh? I thought you told me it was a . . . done deal.

Paul No. I know nothing.

Pause.

Michel Can I ask you a question? Just that, if I understood correctly, before she admitted this 'affair' to you, you'd told her yourself that you'd cheated on her . . . Is that right?

Paul Yes.

Michel You never mentioned it to me.

Paul What?

Michel The fact you were seeing someone else.

Paul Why should I have told you about it? It's completely unimportant.

Michel I am your friend, after all.

Paul You're not going to get annoyed about it!

64

Michel No, but what I'd say to you is those kinds of secrets, you're better off telling a friend, rather than your wife . . .

Paul I know.

Michel I can't understand why you told her you'd cheated on her! It's completely idiotic.

Paul She pressed me so hard that, I don't know, I finished up telling her the truth.

Michel This whole problem springs from that, old man. It's the basic rule, isn't it? *Never tell your wife the truth.*

Paul I know. I can't imagine what came over me.

Pause.

Michel And then, this morning, when she woke up, she suddenly announced she'd had an affair with another man. Is that it?

Paul And what's more, with someone I know.

Michel What makes you say that?

Paul She said: 'Who do you think?' I asked her who it was and her answer was: 'Who do you think?' So I know him.

Michel starts laughing, though he's trying to control his laughter.

What? Why are you laughing?

Michel No reason. Sorry.

Paul Yes. Tell me.

Pause.

Do you know who it is?

Michel Paul . . .

Paul Michel? If you know who it is, tell me.

Michel Yesterday evening, you were maintaining the opposite.

Paul What?

Michel You were saying that friendship called for lying in this type of situation. Remember?

Paul So you do know who it is?

Michel (*as if it were self-evident*) Yes.

Paul Tell me . . .

Pause.

Michel . . .

Michel What?

Paul I'm asking you to tell me.

Michel It's obvious. Isn't it?

Paul I don't want to play guessing-games, Michel. So? Who is it?

Michel It's nobody.

Paul What?

Michel I mean, honestly, just think for a minute! Her story doesn't begin to stand up. She's never cheated on you.

Paul But I just told you . . .

Michel (*interrupting him*) No, no! She simply invented the story to . . .

Paul To what?

Michel As revenge, Paul. I mean, open your eyes . . . You bluntly admitted you'd been deceiving her for months! She was hurt. She wanted revenge.

66

Paul She's not like that.

Michel All women are like that.

Paul You think?

Michel Obviously. And the proof is, when you asked her who it was, her answer was: 'Who do you think?'

Paul Meaning?

Michel She only said that to make you suffer. So that you would start torturing yourself, imagining all the possibilities . . . Which, by the way, you did. No, it's pure vengeance. And it won't end there, you'll see . . .

Paul What do you mean?

Michel She's going to go on lying to you. And she'll even, I don't know, try to make you believe she's slept with . . . I don't know . . . She'll say whatever hurts you the most . . . I bet she'll tell you she's slept with your brother.

Paul I don't have a brother.

Michel Well, then, all right, I don't know . . . With me!

Paul What?

Michel Or something along those lines.

Paul She'd never say that. She's not stupid.

Michel That's not what I was saying.

Paul She'd never make up anything as implausible as that.

Michel Why is it so implausible?

Paul Really, Michel . . . You had dinner with us yesterday . . .

Michel Exactly . . . She could easily tell you that, yes, for several months now, she'd been having an affair with me behind your back.

Paul No . . .

Michel Why not? These things happen, you know. Let's imagine . . . This affair had been going on for several months, but three weeks ago, well, a little less than three weeks ago, she'd decided to put a stop to it. Overnight, she'd decided she didn't want to see me any more, or answer my messages, or respond when my name appeared on her mobile . . . So, suffering from a kind of amorous pique, I'd persuaded you to organise a dinner party at your place. Because it was my idea, remember?

Paul What idea?

Michel The idea of the dinner party. I'd only have done that to see her again. To try to convince her not to break off so abruptly. It was only a pretext to see her again. You follow?

Paul Stop it, I'm serious, Michel . . .

Michel So am I.

Brief pause. A moment of uncertainty.

What I'm trying to say to you is that that could easily have been the truth . . . After all. Do you remember when she left the room yesterday evening, remember?

Paul Yes.

Michel She left for the kitchen, quite brutally, to convey her displeasure . . . I went and joined her. True? Who's to say it wasn't so that I could have a private word with her?

Brief pause.

Who's to say it wasn't to try to convince her not to break off like that, overnight, with no explanation? Can you believe it? Not a word of explanation! It was really brutal.

Paul Yes, I understand the scenario, Michel. Believe me, it's not at all plausible.

Michel No?

Paul No. Because the problem arose from the fact she'd just seen you kissing another girl in the street . . .

Michel Might not be true. How do you know? Perhaps it was just a pretext for cancelling the dinner. As I just said, she didn't want to see me any more.

Paul No, no . . . She's never going to invent a thing like that. Not about you, Michel. Never about you!

Michel (*pretending to be annoyed*) Why don't you come right out and say I'm not a suitable lover for your wife?

Paul laughs.

You see, now you're laughing about it . . .

Paul All the same, I assure you I don't have the stomach to laugh at this.

Michel Yes, you do. I'm telling you her story doesn't stand up for a minute. No better than mine. She lied to you, quite simply, and as for you, you're an idiot for telling her the truth.

Paul I know.

Michel She lied to you. Believe me. None of it was true.

Paul If only that were true . . .

Michel But it *is* true, none of it was true.

Paul Hm . . .

Michel She lied to you because you told her the truth. It's as simple as that.

Paul You mean, it's not true?

Michel (*all in one breath*) She's never cheated on you, Paul, believe me, I'm not mistaken, you mustn't believe her when she tells you she's cheated on you, I'm telling you the truth, she's lying.

Paul Hm.

Paul looks a bit lost. Pause.

Thanks for explaining all that. Because I was a bit confused . . .

Michel puts a hand on his shoulder.

Michel Think nothing of it, old man. Think nothing of it.

Pause. Paul seems confused. Contradictory ideas jostle in his mind. Blackout.

Six

The living room. Paul is waiting for Alice. He looks exhausted. The door opens. She comes in.

Alice It's me.

She steps into the room. Long silence.

It went well, actually. In case you were wondering . . .

Pause.

I'm talking about my presentation. In front of the whole commission.

Paul What did they say?

Alice All positive.

Paul They're going to accept the project?

Alice Definitely, yes.

Paul Good.

Brief pause.

Congratulations.

Alice Thank you.

Pause.

Paul You must be pleased . . .

Alice Exhausted, more than anything.

Pause.

What about you?

Paul Oh, I've had a wonderful day! I spent several hours on the sofa thinking over your announcement this morning, but otherwise, apart from that, you know, everything's fine! Thanks for asking.

Pause.

Alice Paul . . .

Paul What?

Alice You know very well I said the first thing that came into my head.

Brief pause.

I've never had a relationship with another man.

Paul That's not what you said this morning . . .

Alice I was making it up.

Paul Is that true?

Alice (*as if it were obvious, almost amused by his naivety*) Yes.

Pause.

Paul So you lied to me?

Alice I've just told you.

Paul But why?

Alice Why do you think?

Pause.

Paul I'm finding it hard to believe you.

Alice And yet I believed you when you told me you'd made it all up. You know, your 'fantastical' story . . . You did say it wasn't true . . . That you'd made it all up . . . Didn't you? That was it, wasn't it? I have got this right? Well, it's the same for me. I made it all up.

Paul You don't think it might be time to stop lying to each other?

Alice I thought lying was a sign of love.

Paul Let's say I was wrong about that.

Pause.

I'm asking you to tell me the truth.

Alice What truth?

Paul You know very well. The story you told me this morning . . .

Pause.

I've been going crazy all day, you know. It's been the worst day of my life.

Alice I can imagine.

Pause.

Apparently Michel came to see you.

Paul Yes. I needed to talk to somebody. I told him what had happened. He had a better theory about why you were so unpleasant yesterday evening. But you know what the real laugh is?

Alice No.

Paul It wasn't him in the street! Can you believe it? It's true he talked to me about this girl . . . The one who did his head in . . . It's ancient history. He doesn't see her any more.

Alice He doesn't?

Paul No. It's over. He told me just now . . . So, you see? It wasn't them you saw in the street . . . Don't you think that's a laugh?

Alice What?

Paul All these discussions, all these arguments . . . All that for *nothing*!

Alice Not for nothing. At least we've told each other the truth.

Paul So is that the truth?

Pause. She doesn't say no.

Alice? What are you trying to do? You want to torture me, is that it?

Pause.

I just want you to explain.

Alice Explain what?

Paul What happened.

Pause.

Tell me.

Alice 'I've forgotten.'

Paul You see, you're toying with me.

Alice Not at all.

Pause.

Paul Who was it? Do I know him?

Pause.

Why won't you answer?

Alice Because in certain circumstances I think it's best not to say anything. There's a word for that, isn't there? It's on the tip of my tongue . . . What is it again? Oh, yes, that's it . . . 'tact' . . .

Paul Why are you doing this?

Alice Out of love, my love.

Paul There's only one thing you can do out of love: tell me the truth.

Alice You mean to say you're asking me as 'a sign of love'?

Paul Stop it, I'm begging you . . .

Pause.

You can't do this to me. You've no right to . . .

Pause.

Can't you see the state I'm in?

Pause.

Alice All right.

Pause.

You're sure you want to know?

Pause.

You really want to?

Paul Yes.

Alice I don't really see the point, but since you want to know the details . . . All right, then . . .

*Pause. Hiatus. She takes on a confessional tone.
Everything that follows is painfully sincere. Suddenly,
all the lightness has disappeared. It has to be impossible
not to believe her.*

It started six months ago.

Paul What?

Alice It just landed on me. I was completely taken by surprise, you know. I never thought it would happen to me. At first I resisted. Believe me, I resisted.

Paul Who was it?

Alice I stupidly thought I wasn't that kind of woman. As if that could mean anything . . . But it was stronger than me and I let myself be carried away. It was very painful. I'm not saying it was *all* painful. Obviously, there were joyful moments. But there were also hours of misery. I was torn apart. I think you must have suspected sometimes. Didn't you?

Paul No.

Alice If I'm using the past tense, it's because it's finished now.

Paul But who was it?

Pause. She doesn't answer.

Alice It wasn't easy. I mean, finishing. I've tried several times, because of the guilt, but we always came back to one another.

Paul But who are you talking about?

Alice But then, three weeks ago, well, a little less than three weeks ago, I realised it wasn't possible any more. I couldn't do it any more. Something had broken. The spell. The sense of destiny. I don't know. Yes, suddenly it became dazzlingly clear to me how absurd the situation was and I succeeded in breaking it off. You have to believe me. From now on, all that belongs in the past.

Pause.

Paul Do I know him?

Alice Yes.

Paul Who is he?

Alice What's it matter?

Paul (*more insistently*) Who is he?

Pause.

If you don't tell me, I'll never be able to trust you again. Do you realise that?

Pause.

Who is he?

Alice I thought he'd come here to tell you himself.

Paul Who?

Alice Michel.

Pause.

Paul Sorry?

Pause.

Sorry. You're telling me that . . . this whole story you've just told me is about Michel?

Alice Yes.

Paul Michel?

Pause. He still can't believe it.

Wait a minute, wait a minute . . . When you say 'Michel', you mean *my* Michel?

Pause. He suddenly bursts out laughing.

Alice What? What's so funny? Why are you laughing?

Paul No, I'm sorry. Oh, my God! I was so scared, darling.

Alice What are you talking about?

Paul If you knew, darling . . . If you knew how scared I was.

He embraces her.

Alice I'm delighted you're taking it like this.

Paul You almost had me, you know?

Alice Did I?

Paul Yes. I've spent a horrendous day. I imagined every single possibility. It was ghastly. I even imagined you'd slept with old Hervon! Can you imagine? I was going crazy. Old Hervon! Oh, darling . . .

He looks at her, his expression intense, and strokes her cheek.

I adore you.

Alice Why are you looking at me like that?

Paul I'm thinking you must really be angry with me to make up something like this. Michel? My best friend? I can just imagine it! You and Michel! My God . . .

Alice What?

Paul I did suspect you might have made all this up to get back at me, but I never imagined you could be this cruel . . .

Alice It's true, Paul.

Paul (*not believing her*) Course it is.

Alice I'm telling you it's true!

Paul (*thinking he'll catch her out*) Oh, yes? I thought you caught him yesterday in the arms of another woman? Didn't you?

Pause. He's pleased with himself.

Now you don't know what to say . . .

Alice I . . .

Paul (*interrupting her*) I see, of course! Now you're going to tell me it was only a pretext to cancel the dinner, that you never did see him in the arms of another woman . . . Is that it? That you made it all up . . . Tell me, do you really take me for an idiot or what?

Alice Not at all.

Paul So?

She doesn't immediately answer. He smiles.

I'm cleverer than I look, you know.

Alice It is true. I did in fact see him kissing a woman in the street.

Paul (*thinking he's scored a point*) Ah!

He believes his reasoning is untouchable.

Alice That's exactly why I reacted the way I did.

Brief pause. He frowns.

It's not even three weeks since we stopped seeing each other. I know it was my decision. But that doesn't alter the fact that . . . Less than three weeks, can you imagine? What a bastard!

Paul What?

Alice I was disgusted. Do you understand? And then that he accepted to come here . . . I didn't think he'd go that far. To come to my flat. To make protestations of love to his wife, in front of me, with the sole intention of provoking me . . .

Paul I don't believe you.

Alice It drove me crazy.

Paul That's why you got up and left so brutally?

Alice When I went to the kitchen, he rushed to come with me. He tried to kiss me. But I told him I'd seen him with another woman . . . Naturally, he pretended I'd made a mistake, that I'd mixed him up with someone else, that there was no one else in his life, that he still loved me . . .

Paul You're lying, Alice.

Alice But I knew it was him. I passed right by him in the taxi. I couldn't have made a mistake. I recognised him! What does he think I am, an idiot?

Paul But . . .

Alice But he went on lying. And when I told him that anyway, whether it was him or not, it made no difference to my decision, that I couldn't go on the way we were, because of you, that the guilt was too powerful, he rolled his eyes, as if . . .

Paul As if what?

Alice As if I was deluding myself about you. As if I was naive to imagine you were faithful to me and I had no reason to feel guilty.

Brief pause.

That's why I asked you all those questions after dinner. To find out if he'd done that to get his own back. Or if in fact you'd cheated on me as well.

Pause.

Paul Are you taking the piss?

Pause.

Alice? Just reassure me, you made up this story last night to get back at me?

Pause.

Don't tell me it's true . . .

Pause.

Alice, is it true? You're telling the truth? About Michel?

Pause.

I mean, it's appalling! Do you realise? It's horrible!

Alice You cheated on me as well! Didn't you?

Paul But that's nothing to do with it! I mean, do you realise what you've just told me?

Paul seems completely undone. He bursts into tears.

Alice (*who wasn't at all expecting this reaction*) Paul, what's the matter with you?

Paul I just can't get my head around it.

Alice Don't, Paul . . .

Paul (*through his tears*) I could never have believed . . .

Not wanting to weep in front of Alice, Paul turns on his heel and makes a dash for the bedroom. He closes the door behind him.

Alice Paul, what are you doing? Where are you going? Paul? Open the door . . . Paul? Darling? Don't tell me you believed me? Paul? I was joking. Paul? How stupid are you?

She starts laughing. We start to believe she's been playing a part up to now and that in fact this story about Michel is unlikely. She's convincing.

Can you imagine me sleeping with Michel? You know very well what I think about him. And Laurence is my best friend. Listen, darling, think for two minutes, I was just saying it to . . . How could you believe it was true for one second?

Pause. The door opens.

Paul You haven't slept with Michel?

Alice (*as if it were self-evident*) Of course not.

Paul Do you swear it?

Alice On your head.

Paul But your story . . . this affair . . .

Alice I made it all up. Really, Paul . . . Do you believe everything you're told?

Paul Do you realise how cruel this was? Why did you do it?

Alice Because you spent all evening singing the praises of lying. And all morning lying to me.

Paul I didn't lie to you, Alice. How many times do I have to tell you?

Alice This girl . . .

Paul There never was a girl!

Alice starts laughing. She still doesn't believe him.

I'm telling you, there never was a girl! I didn't spend the night with her. I swear to you. How many more times do I have to say it?

Alice Is that the truth?

Paul The truth is, I love you. And that I would never cheat on you. Never. You have to believe me.

Brief pause.

You have to believe me, if you want me to believe you . . .

Alice I believe you.

Paul Is that true?

Alice Of course. Since you tell me. I understand now that you made up this whole story to . . . Why did you, exactly?

Paul To make you jealous.

Alice That's it.

Paul And also to show you . . .

Alice Yes, yes. That's right.

Paul And to demonstrate that certain kinds of discussion lead directly to fisticuffs.

Alice Of course, darling. Of course I believe you.

Paul That's good.

Alice But you do too?

Paul I do what?

Alice Believe me?

Paul Yes. Shouldn't I?

Alice Yes. You have to believe me.

Paul Yes. Of course I believe you. Of course.

They look at each other as if they've finally rediscovered one another; and they're smiling at each other.

Alice You see how much simpler things are when you tell each other the truth.

Paul Yes, you're right.

Alice You shouldn't ever have to make up stories like that . . .

Paul No. It's idiotic. The last thing I want is to be like those couples . . . You know, those couples who have to lie to one another . . .

Alice (*disgusted expression*) Oh . . . no.

Paul Who never discuss things as they really are. That'd be too depressing.

Alice Yes. No. That's not us.

Paul Not us, no. We deserve better than that.

Alice Yes. Everything's infinitely simpler when you tell each other the truth.

Paul Yes. What proves it . . .

They're trying to convince one another.

Because love is something pure.

Alice Absolutely.

Paul To love someone is to be true. It's to have nothing to hide.

Alice Exactly. It's to be able to tell each other the truth.

Paul Yes. The whole truth.

Alice And nothing but the truth.

They embrace. They're very close now, their intimacy rediscovered.

Paul Ha, it feels like waking out of a long nightmare.

Alice Same for me.

Paul How about a little glass of something to recover from all this emotion?

Alice Good idea . . .

He goes to fetch a bottle and two glasses.

Paul Oh, my God . . . What a day . . .

Alice laughs.

What? What is it?

Alice Nothing. I was thinking of your face when I told you I was sleeping with Michel. How could you have believed something like that?

Paul I don't know . . . That story about the kitchen . . . It had a kind of . . . Then, it only takes a minute before you stop being able to tell the difference between what's true and what isn't . . .

He pours a glass and gives it to her.

Even so, there was one detail that helped me understand it wasn't true, your story about Michel.

Alice Oh, yes?

Paul Yes. A detail which cast a shadow over its credibility.

Alice Really? What was that?

Paul You want to know?

Alice I'm all ears.

He pours himself a glass.

Paul When you told me that, yesterday evening, in the kitchen, Michel implied you'd be wrong to feel guilty about me, because supposedly I wasn't faithful to you . . .

Alice So? What's not believable about that?

Paul He wouldn't have been able to say something like that to you.

Alice Wouldn't he?

Paul No. You know why? Because I never confided in him. By the way, he even complained about it just now . . .

Alice Mm, it's good, this wine.

Paul And do you know why I never mentioned that girl to him, the one last summer? The one in Antibes . . .

Alice (*still smiling*) Stop it . . .

Paul I could have talked about her to any other friend. But to him specifically, it was impossible. And do you know why? Out of 'tact' . . .

Alice laughs. Paul starts laughing also.

What?

Alice Darling, what exactly are you trying to make me believe?

Paul Nothing.

Alice That the girl you *never* had an affair with was Laurence? Is that it? Is that what you're trying to tell me?

Paul is being enigmatic; he doesn't answer.

I appreciate your attempts at revenge, darling.

Paul Really?

Alice Yes. I take your trying to be cruel as a token of your affection.

Paul That's nice of you.

Alice But we made a pact, the two of us . . .

Paul A pact? Did we?

Alice We said we'd tell each other nothing but the truth.

Paul starts laughing.

Paul Yes, it's true.

Alice So stop with your stories . . . Do you mind?

Paul I will stop, sorry.

Alice And anyway, you'll never succeed in making me believe something like that.

Paul Won't I?

Alice No, never.

Paul Then you're right, let's talk about something else . . .

Alice Yes.

Brief pause.

Paul So? Here's to you?

Alice To us, darling.

They clink glasses, smiling at each other. Pause. But suddenly Alice's expression darkens – as if a doubt had overtaken her – while Paul is glowing from this little silent victory.

Blackout.

Lights up.

The actors take their curtain call. It seems to be the end of the performance. But after a few bows, the curtain goes up on a lit set: the four actors have taken their places for the Epilogue.

Seven

Paul, Alice, Michel and Laurence. It's a repeat, but this time the words sound different and seem to carry another meaning.

Laurence I'd never do that.

Alice Why?

Laurence I don't know. You're my friends. I wouldn't want to cause a row between you.

Paul In any case, it's not something that will ever happen. So let's change the subject.

Laurence You never know.

Paul Of course you do. You want me to tell you why? Because, even if sometimes she can be really irritating, I'm completely crazy about my wife.

Michel Me too.

   Brief pause.

I mean about mine, obviously.

   Paul and Laurence laugh. Pause.

The basic problem, Alice, is that whatever they may claim, people don't really want to be told the truth.

Alice Is that what you think?

Michel I know from experience. When I started out, you can't imagine how many writers I infuriated because I made the mistake of telling them honestly what I thought of their manuscripts . . . In the end, every one of them resented me. And I'm prepared to bet this friend of yours,

the one you were telling us about, would wind up
holding it against you, if you told her what you saw.

Alice So lying's the only answer?

Michel Let's say, keeping your secrets.

Alice (*coldly*) Right. I'm going to check the dinner.

She gets up abruptly.

Paul No, don't worry, I'll do it.

Alice No, no. That's all right.

*She goes out. At this point, the wall separating the living
room from the kitchen becomes semi-transparent.
Alice's silhouette can be seen.*

Michel What's the matter with her?

Paul I don't know.

Michel Did I say something?

Paul No, no, I don't think so. She's just gone to check the
dinner, you know, the what-d'you-call-it, the rabbit.

Laurence I'll go and see if she needs a hand.

Paul No! No, not you.

Laurence What?

Michel All right. I'll go. I somehow think it'd be better if
I go . . . Don't you think?

Paul Yes. Maybe.

Michel Let me try and put things right . . . But do you
think it's to do with what I just said?

Paul No. I don't think so.

Michel Fine. I'll go and see. I'll be back.

*He goes out to join Alice in the kitchen. An inaudible
conversation, apparently tempestuous, then begins*

*between them – an argument which clearly belongs in
the category of amorous conflict.*

Laurence What's the matter with her?

Paul She's a bit stressed because of her meeting tomorrow.

Laurence No, seriously . . . Is something going on?

Pause.

What's going on?

*Pause. Laurence and Paul start whispering, through to
the end of the scene.*

You think she suspects?

Paul No, no.

He takes her hand.

Laurence Stop it.

Paul What?

Laurence Not here.

Paul I can't wait, if you only knew.

Laurence Me too . . .

Paul Quiberon. I adore that place . . .

Laurence I hope the weather'll be as good as it was in
Antibes . . .

Paul smiles suggestively.

What did you tell Alice?

Paul I told her I was going to Amiens to meet some
clients.

Laurence No!

Paul Yes.

Laurence She believes you?

Paul Why shouldn't she believe me? I never lie to her.

Laurence Liar.

He smiles. Then kisses her. In the kitchen, Alice repels Michel. She could go so far as to slap him. The two images overlap.

(*While she's kissing him.*) Stop it.

Paul What?

Laurence I'm embarrassed. They're right there.

Paul So?

Laurence It's not right.

Paul I suppose not. Sorry.

Pause.

What are they doing?

Laurence I don't know. You want me to go and see?

Paul Shh, they're coming back.

They spring apart from one another.

You know, just now, when I told you you looked magnificent in that dress, I was telling the truth.

Laurence The *what*?

Paul The truth.

Laurence (*shrugging her shoulders*) Never heard of it.

He smiles. Alice returns. Followed by Michel. Paul gets up. Alice adjusts her dress. A pause full of invisible tensions. Then everybody smiles, as if nothing has happened. Blackout.

Alternatively: a final line from Alice, if it seems necessary to round off the situation.

Alice Right, well, I think we know where we're sitting!